A Painter's Scotla

Late Afternoon, Eigg & Rum   90 x 110 cm   2014

A Painter's Scotland
Favourite Places, Favourite Paintings

Charles Simpson

SIMPSON

For my life with Mary

ISBN 978 0 9552954 5 4

Charles Simpson
Inglecraig
Bowland Road
Clovenfords
Selkirkshire
TD1 3ND

www.csimpson-art.co.uk

Designed and produced by Charles Simpson

Photography of paintings by:
John McKenzie, Gordon Bell, Charles Simpson

Other photography by:
Charles Simpson, Mary Simpson

Printed by Biddles Books Ltd, King's Lynn, Norfolk

Track through the Snow (detail)   30 x 40 cm   2016
Inglecraig and Whytbank from Craig Hill.

Note: all paintings are oil on canvas unless otherwise stated.

Contents

Introduction 7

A Painter's Life 9

Painting 21

Travels 33

Clovenfords, Scottish Borders 45

Arisaig to Mallaig 59

Iona and Mull 71

Islands 87

Achiltibuie & the Summer Isles 107

North West 117

Postscript 144

Dazzling Light, Tanera Mor   90 x 110 cm   2011
Tanera Mor is the largest of the Summer Isles.

Introduction

Probably like any painter, it's difficult to explain why I paint what I paint, why I am drawn to particular subject matter. Perhaps it is an emotional connection or just pure instinct. Certainly I am continually driven to paint my native country, and particularly the north west coast and islands of Scotland. I do paint around my home in the Scottish Borders but to a lesser extent. On the other hand the village of Clovenfords where I live, I find suits my everyday basic needs extremely well. Perhaps I would find it difficult to be based in the north west continuously, and far better for me to have my regular material gathering excursions there.

When I was young my parents took me with my elder brother and sisters on our annual fortnight holidays to rented caravans at the likes of St Andrews, Arbroath and Maidens. One year we had a "two centre" holiday, the first week in Montrose and the second in the more adventurous and far flung Ullapool. While at the latter we visited Gairloch and Achiltibuie. I don't remember much about that holiday, apart from fishing off Ullapool harbour, but I can only assume it somehow made a lasting impression on my young self.

Those nostalgic memories encouraged me to return in my late twenties on a camping holiday with my wife Mary. We have been journeying there ever since, especially once I started painting again in my mid thirties.

I have made painting trips elsewhere. I produced some works from beach holidays in Minorca, Majorca and Fuerteventura in my earlier painting life. I later made more serious trips to Venice (twice) and then Cornwall, both locations resulting in very satisfying paintings. But my painting heart "lies in the highlands", or rather the north west coast and islands to be more accurate.

Deep Snow   80 x 100 cm   2010
Craig Hill, across the road from our house.

A Painter's Life

I have been a full time painter since 1999. That has been my only source of income in that time.

I was born in 1952 in Tullibody, Clackmannanshire, the youngest of four children. Though described as a village, Tullibody was relatively large with three primary schools. It was very much a working class community with very few privately owned houses. George Reid the politician was born there. Local girl Sheena Drummond was crowned Miss UK in 1969. She wore make up and stylish clothes, which was not the norm in Tullibody. I drew all the time as a child, usually knights in armour, cowboys, ships, aeroplanes and battles. My dad liked to draw Andy Capp the strip cartoon character. I was always top of my class at primary.

I went on to Alloa Academy the senior secondary for Clackmannanshire. In fifth year I had the unusual distinction of winning both the art and maths prizes. I was greatly encouraged, particularly in sixth year, by my art teacher John White – who a few years later tragically died in an unlikely accident. In my first year at Glasgow School of Art I realised just how good some of the other students were. Many of them seemed much more sophisticated, worldly wise and experienced than me. Some male students even had beards.

I graduated from Glasgow School of Art in 1975 with a BA in graphic design. I had given up the painting course as I found it too frustrating and switched to graphic design. After college I worked as a graphic designer in Edinburgh including five years at Churchill Livingstone medical publishers. I moved from there to run the graphics department of Wood Mackenzie, a large Edinburgh stockbroker. It was quite a change after the calm and polite world of publishing. I was thrown in at the deep end, having to learn about using computers and then setting up page make-up production processes. I worked long hours and it could be very intense. I was stuck there for eight years and realised I had to give up my day job for the sake of my soul!

After some discussion Mary and I put our house on the market with the aim of downsizing, my leaving full time employment and working for myself. A sale was agreed after six weeks. That was a Friday in November 1990. On the Sunday we drove down the Borders and stumbled upon "Inglecraig". It was a small cottage in a poor state but perfect for our needs. On the Wednesday morning the purchase had been finalised. I could start to plan handing in my notice but that same day I was remarkably made redundant, along with several others. I was home by lunchtime with a most unexpected and very useful cheque. In the stockbroking world redundancy was normally a fairly brutal experience where redundancees were escorted straight out the front door. However, I couldn't believe my luck! The following day I even had a freelance design project to begin. In March 1991 we moved from our shiny new house in Edinburgh to our small country cottage in Clovenfords.

While at Wood Mackenzie, as a more creative outlet, I had started painting small watercolours and gouaches and eventually oils. I had

Farm near Linlithgow   gouache   20 x 30 cm   1987

Farm in Winter, Kirkbrae   acrylic   28 x 40 cm   1990

Early days at Inglecraig, 1991

We often found frogs in the wooden rear porch. Down the side of the house were a couple of old sheds and a tumbledown fence which included assorted tv aerials and *Daily Record* signs as additional support.

Inglecraig with the new studio on the left, winter 2004

begun exhibiting in a very small way but the income was quite modest. Graphic design, mainly book design for my old employer Churchill Livingstone, became my bread and butter. However that first year I had my first serious exhibition at the Macaulay Gallery in Stenton, East Lothian.

Mary was doing some reflexology and massage work from the cottage and together we struggled by with some good times but also several difficult periods. After another show at Macaulay I then had two successful exhibitions at The Open Eye in Edinburgh. I had started to show and sell in London and painting was proving a more rewarding route than the declining design work. In 1999 I decided to start painting full-time. I also wanted to try a different approach and so in 2000 rented the Dundas Street Gallery below Bourne Fine Art in Edinburgh. I put on a solo exhibition for two weeks with myself and Mary staffing the gallery. Despite not having any contacts or mailing list, the exhibition did very well. We staged further exhibitions there in 2001, 2002 and 2004.

It was a most rewarding experience and a great deal was learned about putting on exhibitions and dealing with gallery visitors. We formed some good and lasting relationships with a few clients. One gentleman from Darlington drove up for the day every show to buy a painting. All the shows sold consistently well and with just a few expenses we earned some very useful income.

Despite successful shows at Dundas Street Gallery I realised that expansion possibilities were limited and if I wanted to develop my painting I needed a bigger, more challenging stage. In those years I had formed a good relationship with Bourne Fine Art. Patrick Bourne had been an encouraging mentor but Bourne had just merged with The Fine Art Society and he was now moving to become its overall managing director in London. With Emily Walsh taking over in Edinburgh it seemed an appropriate moment for me to "move upstairs".

They were ten very good years at Bourne and it was an excellent fit for me at that stage. Due to its specialist nature it did not stage many

Bourne Fine Art, Edinburgh 2007

Cork Street Gallery, London 2010

Bourne Fine Art, Edinburgh 2011

Bourne Fine Art, Edinburgh 2012 (sixtieth birthday exhibition)

Panter & Hall, London, 2012

The Scottish Gallery, Edinburgh 2015

The Scottish Gallery, Edinburgh 2015

The Scottish Gallery, Edinburgh 2015

individual exhibitions and they were able to be more flexible than many other commercial galleries. I was actually one of the small number of gallery artists who were not dead! Apart from five solo exhibitions they indulged me with my idea for a very different sixtieth birthday show. I had also approached Bourne about renting the Cork Street Gallery in London and that exhibition also proved successful despite the high rental costs and accommodation. At Bourne I gained great experience in crafting and theming a big exhibition, something which I now particularly enjoy. After my exhibition there in 2014 I instinctively realised that with their small specialist mailing list, it was perhaps an opportune moment for change.

After agreement with Emily at Bourne Fine Art I was most fortunate that Guy Peploe at The Scottish Gallery, just down the road, was interested in taking me on as a gallery artist. I had my first solo show there in 2015. The Scottish Gallery's history, reputation and professionalism speak for themselves, both in Scotland and the UK. As a gallery it provides unique support and opportunity for its artists. I have been most privileged to show in two such beautiful spaces in Edinburgh.

Galleries tend to allocate solo exhibitions to their artists every two years. Consequently my painting cycle, for want of a better description, begins with or focuses on my Edinburgh exhibition. I have always done well in Edinburgh and that for me has been the creative trigger or drive to what I will be painting. I exhibit in London, originally with Ainscough Contemporary Art and since 2003 with Panter & Hall where I have had seven solo exhibitions to date. I have also shown with John Davies Gallery in the Cotswolds. I concentrate on solo exhibitions and do like a big space. I don't do much in the way of mixed shows or submit work to the big annual shows (RSW, RGI, SSA etc) or open competitions.

It is not always a secure life being a painter but not many people are able to make a living doing something they love, something they would be doing anyway. The downside is financial dependability. Income is irregular and unpredictable while expenditure such as framing and materials must carry on regardless if work is to continue, even when times might be difficult. It is one of those jobs where the work must be done first, hoping that someone will buy it – and there are no guarantees of that happening. There is also the long term issue of trying to provide for a private pension. Work is very solitary where the artist must set their own standards and not be swayed by external influences. Over the years I have found the act of painting itself has become the most important factor rather than the distractions of self image, popularity, awards or prizes. Selling paintings allows the artist to continue painting, as well as to live. I have also found myself becoming less interested in foreign travel or city visits and, while not wishing to become isolated, I am now far more content with an apparently smaller world where I can concentrate on the things important to me.

When finances were good we invested in our cottage. It may be small (our kitchen is *very* small) but is ideal for the two of us and for my work. We are surrounded by rough fields and hills, open spaces and big skies. The garden is large and includes my separate studio which I built sixteen years ago. Apart from painting I gild and finish frames there. It is also home to our freezer! I have an old wooden garage (200 yards round the corner) which has been transformed into the framing workshop, where the mouldings get cut, joined, painted and sanded. The house and

Inglecraig in Snow
oil on board
20 x 40 cm   1992

Studio, 2017

surroundings truly reflect Mary and myself and the quiet life we lead. I should also add that Mary, whom I have known since I was seventeen and she fifteen, is apart from being my other vital half, my greatest supporter. She has an excellent knowledge of painting and art and is willing to listen and contribute to my obsession with painting and the art world.

Mary and I came to Clovenfords so that we could spend as much of our lives together as we could. Full-time employment interfered with that! The idea to come here wasn't originally so that I could paint. That was only a vague dream. At the time I couldn't possibly have thought that I might one day be exhibiting paintings in The Scottish Gallery or Bourne Fine Art. There are many practical things involved in our everyday lives apart from painting. I make all our bread, do a lot of cooking and I indulge in my Daily Telegraph. We like to get out for a walk and there is always admin work and online ordering etc. Then there are spells of

Crail Shore   60 x 60 cm   2015

framing, gilding, assembling canvases in frames and wrapping finished pictures for sending off to galleries.

I don't know other painters or belong to organisations or groups. I don't have many opportunities to talk about painting and art except with Mary or perhaps when visiting a gallery. I don't like wasting my time. I'm very happy watching some TV or a dvd in the evening, or having an occasional coffee or glass of wine with friends or visitors in an afternoon. But I'm not one for dinner parties or social events. There are obvious long term commitments with exhibitions and also daily ones. Health and welfare are always priorities. In 2016 Mary and I spent nearly three months selling her mother's house in Edinburgh and moving her down to a nice bungalow in the village to be near us. I did little if any work during that time. I prefer a free diary where possible and let the day take care of itself. There is always plenty to do, but I try to avoid being too "busy". Busyness often seems to be seen as a desirable attribute these days.

When time allows I get out to the studio for a few hours, or even just for half an hour. It is important to keep a painting moving on every day. It can be difficult to get back into that painting groove if progress is disturbed. Painting is always in my head, last thing at night and first thing in the morning. If there is a nagging practical issue to be dealt with, I do find it difficult to paint. There are times when everything goes well and I get on a "roll". That's a great time when the painting flows more easily, often when I'm involved in big canvases. I pace myself when working for exhibitions and have enough experience to get things done in plenty of time. I do try to get the work done early and avoid a late rush. I find it always preferable to have plenty of space in my life in order to paint.

October Light, Aberlady   100 x 130 cm   2012
This is the bird reserve on the River Forth at Aberlady. This is one of my favourite paintings as well as being an unexpected and unusual location for me.

Painting

Painting is my job – that's what I do for a living. I aim to be professional in my dealings with galleries and clients and try to utilise my graphic design training and organisation. I tend to be very organised anyway. But painting is much more than that and achieving a balance between being true to your painting self and the commercial world can be tricky, especially when there is a need to produce a volume of work in a specified time for a selling exhibition. Some painters do have a certain amount of safeguard, perhaps with some other income coming into the household or maybe early retiral and with a certain of amount of regular pension. Unfortunately because of the way I came into painting I haven't had any safety net. But I have survived some difficult years and am now at a stage where I can relax somewhat and enjoy and indulge more in my painting.

Though mainly a landscape and seascape painter, I have always been interested in a range of subject matter within that broad spectrum. It keeps me more stimulated and my work fresher. I have at times ventured out of my comfort zone perhaps with small still life studies and even figures. What I paint greatly depends on what I find on my travels or come across at home. I try to keep an open mind so that I can respond to what I see, rather than search for specific images – as I did when I started out. Of course I do return to favourite subjects and locations but hope to tackle them slightly differently if possible. It is difficult for instance not to be drawn back to the north end of Iona again and again.

I have found this varied approach can work for and against the "commercial" or "jobbing" painter as I sometimes describe my job. For instance, some people love snow pictures while others just do not like to be reminded of cold weather! Paintings are also bought for an assortment of different reasons. It may be a specific or general subject or an interest in a particular location; or a painting might evoke emotional

Painting in the front room "studio" (also office and stored the vacuum cleaner)

Painting in the outside studio

or romantic memories such as a childhood holiday. Others buy simply because they like it as a painting. The reputation or standing of the artist plays a part, which may be reflected in the price being paid, as well as the gallery and its reputation in which a painting is displayed. The very successful artist Ken Howard suggested that good work looks poorer in poor company, and better when shown beside good paintings.

I see many very fine painters finding difficulty selling. There are also painters who produce a steady stream of stereotyped work and sell extremely well. Perhaps there is a certain safety value for the purchaser or having a picture by that artist is a fashionable must have. It's difficult to really predict who and what will steadily sell. I have been fortunate. Because of the variety that I produce I have known of potential buyers waiting for quite a spell before a suitable painting became available. I have also had some buyers who have continued to collect a number of paintings over the years, perhaps because of that variety. A London lawyer initially bought a painting at one of my Dundas Street Gallery exhibitions and she now has over 35 paintings of a range of sizes and subject. She has a very good instinctive eye and has some of my favourite paintings.

Subject matter collected during my travels determines what will be painted over the following year or two. The shape and form of exhibitions depends on this material, even down to sizes of paintings. Only certain subjects suit a large scale while small paintings require quite a different approach. The smallest paintings are best if they can exude a certain amount of charm and freshness. The biggest paintings need to have impact, a wow factor if you like, and a certain gravitas.

Every painting presents different issues and may need a slightly different approach or variation in technique and application of paint. I am not one for stylisation or formulaic solutions. Each painting grows by itself. Sometimes I'm not really sure what is going on and it is only experience which enables a route to be found through to the finished picture. Some paintings take me by surprise and are finished quicker than I would

expect. But some are unexpectedly difficult and occasionally it becomes clear that it is just not going to work.

Painting is a series of continuous decisions: what to do next or how to tackle a part of the canvas. Bold decisions are required at times. Painting can be quite intimidating and I can find many other distracting things to do! I'm not a nine till five painter and try to keep my painting fresh. I tend to work on only one painting at a time no matter its size. I do spend quite a bit of time just looking at an ongoing work and then thinking about it when not in the studio.

A painter will always try to produce their best work and hopefully all works shown would be to that standard. Every so often however, a better painting will result – when a painting will go to that next level, or go "somewhere different" as I often describe it. I don't really know what that is or how to define it. The painting just has that extra something, perhaps whereby it exists almost independently of its subject. For

Winter Crow
20 x 20 cm   2011

One of my personal favourite paintings which I have kept. I don't choose to keep many paintings. I can't really say why I like this picture so much. The paintings that I especially like aren't necessarily the most popular or among the better sellers.

instance, I find that the large sea paintings by Joan Eardley take me to that extra place. At times I do produce a painting that goes to that different place and that is a most satisfying feeling. But that does not necessarily mean that particular painting will be seen in the same way by the viewing public. The aim is to produce more if not all paintings to that mysterious level.

I do all my own framing. The finished product has certainly evolved since I started. 25 years ago I would buy in stock mouldings and using a hand mitre saw would cut, join and assemble the frame on the floor of my front room. I progressed to building a large shed at the side of the house and investing in a second hand Morso guillotine and an underpinner. I started to buy bare wooden mouldings but then had the additional complication of learning how to treat and decorate the frames. It took me several years to develop suitable techniques and finishes.

The shed had to be knocked down when I built my studio and the framing workshop moved into the my old garage. Mike is my trusty helper and framer who works in there, chopping and joining mouldings, filling, sanding, painting, wet sanding and polishing with wire wool. Like me he is untrained as a framer but has worked with me for nearly ten years. The old wooden building has no electricity or running water. But we have added extra windows, a gas heater and led lighting using old car batteries for power. When the double doors are opened there is even "double glazing" of a wooden frame with stretched polythene over the opening – our own custom solution to let in the light but keep out the wind! It's actually a very relaxing place to work with a nice outlook over the fields and hills.

I would not describe myself as a picture framer as I do not have the wide set of skills akin to a professional framer. However I do now produce framing which I feel presents and compliments my work as I wish it

Mike in the framing garage/workshop

Dark Evening
30 x 40 cm   2017
Frame gilded in 12ct
gold

to. I devised my own plain wood mouldings and get them supplied to
order. I finish frames in my studio using 12ct gold leaf and coats of matt
wax varnish. It's a deal of work at times but I enjoy it and I find it very
satisfying to see my paintings in my own hand crafted frames. It also
saves a great deal of expenditure on professional framers.

When I was at Glasgow School of Art in the early 1970s it had a
remarkable group of painting tutors who were an enormous and lasting
influence on the "painterliness" of painters who came out of college
during that era. Most influential was David Donaldson the head of
painting. The staff also included James Robertson, Geoffrey Squire,
John Cunningham, Leon Morrocco and Duncan Shanks. Even though
I had moved to graphic design I still consider myself a product of that
painting time. One only has to look at painters who graduated around

then such as Archie Forrest, Glen Scouller, James Fullarton, Joe Hargan and Helen Wilson to see that influence.

I am a great admirer of the work of David Donaldson. He painted quite intuitively and without preparatory work. He drew with a brush and developed the work on the canvas. He would change his technique to suit the subject, whether it be portrait, landscape, still life, nude or biblical story. There was a marvellous retrospective at the Talbot Rice in 1996 just before he died. Possibly my all time personal favourite painting is his *Annette and the Elders* (1980–81).

Joan Eardley has been another big influence on my work. I found the large retrospective at the RSA in 2007 quite inspiring and emotional, particularly the room full of her large seascapes. I love the freedom and application of paint. She had some interesting dynamic ideas on composition which are not always appreciated. Like Donaldson she painted subjects which were very familiar to her.

My other big painting hero is the American Andrew Wyeth. At the last count I had nine books about him. His biography by Richard Meryman is the most inspiring and entertaining art book I have read. Wyeth was a strange though fascinating character, totally committed and obsessed with his work. He also painted subjects with which he was totally familiar, namely the people and countryside where he lived. I loved that he painted a local house and described it as a "portrait" (*Weatherside*, 1965). Fantastically skilled in drawing, drybrush and tempera, he was lauded with honorary degrees and honours but often derided by critics as a romantic photorealist. He actually described himself as a conceptual painter. There were always ideas and personal meanings behind his paintings but he did not think it important that the viewer understand his thinking. I often find great emotion and intensity in his paintings.

Another worthwhile read is *Man with a Blue Scarf* by Martin Gayford, describing his sitting for a portrait by Lucien Freud. Freud again was such an intense character and painter. His paintings can be uncompromising and uneasy on the eye but I do find some of his work

quite stunning such as *Benefits Supervisor Resting* (1994) and *Two Irishmen in W11* (1984).

I have an extensive collection of exhibition catalogues and art books and this is important to my work. I don't think I or other painters need be directly influenced by other artists but it is the looking and examination that is important. It keeps alive that sense of inquiry. I pay attention online to what is being shown in galleries throughout the country and conveniently can visit the Edinburgh galleries on a regular basis. I do have a preferential interest in Scottish painting. I love Guthrie's *The Hind's Daughter* in the Scottish National Gallery and also Patterson's *Autumn in Glencairn*.

When I was about 15 or 16 I went to see the RSA in Edinburgh and here I found work by James McIntosh Patrick for the first time and I was so impressed. Once I started at art school, in my new found wisdom I decided his work somewhat sugary and cloying. When I became a painter in later life I started to appreciate his draughtsmanship and skill again but also the incredible complexity and cleverness of composition.

I always look out for the work of Robin Phillipson, especially his *Women Observed* series, as well as that of Archie Forrest, Duncan Shanks, James

Morrison, Barbara Rae, Frances Walker, Leon Morrocco, Helen Wilson, Gordon Bryce, Alexander Fraser and Sandy Murphy. I do lean towards a painterly realistic style but I admit to being taken by surprise by an exhibition at The Scottish Gallery in 2016 of Wilhelmina Barns-Graham, a stunning display of controlled colour, balance and abstraction.

As with Lucien Freud, Euan Uglow was another powerfully intense painter, though he was painstakingly slow. Other painters from south of the border I find of great interest are Andrew Gifford, the prolific Kurt Jackson and the late Patrick George. Peter Blake has also been a long time hero of mine and I well remember a lecture by him while I was at Glasgow Art School. He always seems like such a nice unassuming man. His *Self Portrait with Badges* of 1961 is such a great picture. He also freely admits a dislike for drawing from life and will generally work from photographs, even tracing directly from them – something that artists are just not meant to do. Whatever it takes!

Ken Howard, Fred Cumming and the late Bernard Dunstan and John Ward are painters that I studied when I started painting. Royal Academicians and members of the new English Art Club, their work, though incredibly popular, is probably now considered old fashioned. But their draughtsmanship and traditional painting skills are worthy of study by the aspiring painter. Anyone who has read Ken Howard's autobiography *Light and Dark* could not fail to be impressed by his dedication and work ethic. I was visiting The Fine Art Society in London at the time of John Ward's final exhibition there and Patrick Bourne kindly introduced me to him. It was quite a moment for me to meet such a gentlemanly painter that I had admired for so long.

I do think that for the young painter there is much to be learned and appreciated from observing older more experienced painters. Morrison and Shanks are Scottish painters I have always paid more attention to. They have forged long term careers through working quietly, honestly and diligently and have done so being faithful to their work and true to themselves.

Starlings & Buttercups, Iona   40 x 40 cm   2015

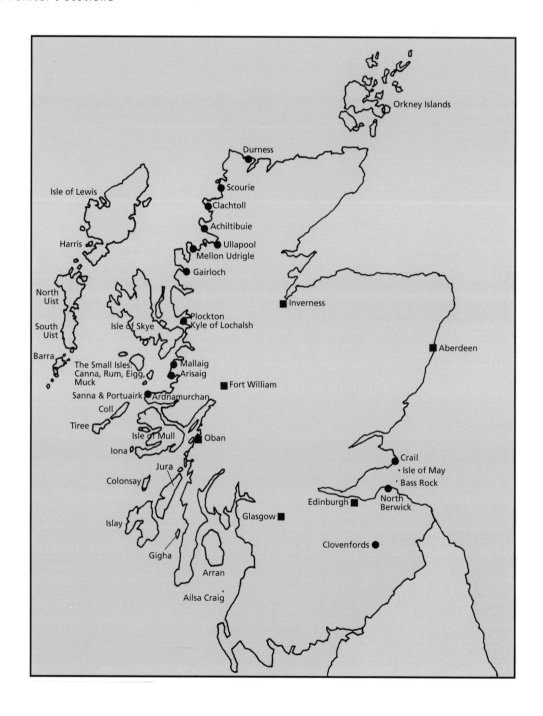

Orkney Islands

Durness

Isle of Lewis

Scourie

Clachtoll

Achiltibuie

Harris

Ullapool
Mellon Udrigle

Gairloch

North
Uist

Inverness

South
Uist

Plockton
Kyle of Lochalsh

Isle of Skye

Barra

Aberdeen

The Small Isles:
Canna, Rum, Eigg,
Muck

Mallaig
Arisaig

Sanna & Portuairk

Fort William

Ardnamurchan

Coll

Tiree

Isle of Mull

Oban

Iona

Crail

Jura

• Isle of May
• Bass Rock

Colonsay

Edinburgh

North
Berwick

Islay

Glasgow

Gigha

Clovenfords

Arran

Ailsa Craig

Travels

There are two problems travelling and holidaying in north west Scotland, namely midges and unpredictable weather. Apart from protective clothing, sprays, creams and evasion, we can do nothing much about the former, but the weather's unpredictability and changeability somehow makes Scotland what it is. The most spectacular day I ever had on Iona was when we crossed over on the ferry from Fionnphort with what looked like a nasty storm approaching from Jura. It did not look very encouraging but Mary and I walked on up to the north beach. When we got there the sky suddenly cleared and the sun burst through while the waves were pounding in.

I do have an intense dislike of midges while they seem to have a passionate liking for me. I moved on from camping mainly because of our little Scottish friends. However, over the years they have not been

Mallaig to Armadale
ferry, 2015

as much of a problem as their fearsome reputation suggests, only on a few occasions. Just don't go walking near woods or water in warm damp weather. The west coast usually has a good breeze anyway. On a positive note, if not for midges and the weather, northern Scotland might be far too busy for my liking.

The first journey Mary and I undertook together was in 1975 when we travelled by train from Edinburgh to Scrabster and then by a very windy ferry to Stromness. We had set off with our small tent (purchased through a "club book" as it was known), sleeping bags from Woolworths and our redoubtable cagoules to protect against the weather. We walked from the ferry to the Stromness campsite, pitched camp and then I succeeded in bursting the gas canister. We had a meal of orange squash and jam sandwiches. Edinburgh had been hot and sunny when we left but Orkney was much colder even though it was summer. We were totally unprepared and had to buy an extra sleeping bag and Mary a pair of gloves. We travelled about by public bus though we did take a bus tour to Skara Brae, Maeshowe and the Ring of Brodgar. We had a great trip despite our naivety.

That same year we booked a last minute cottage in Arisaig through an ad in The Scotsman. We took a train from Edinburgh to Glasgow, another

Stromness campsite, Orkney, 1975

Cottage, Arisaig, 1975

to Fort William and then the small local train to Arisaig on the Mallaig line over the spectacular Glenfinnan viaduct – long before Harry Potter. The white cottage sat round the bay from Arisaig. It was very basic and the wallpaper moved when the wind blew. The owner, very much a local shall we say, had been to Edinburgh once but didn't like all the buses. We took the train to Mallaig a few times and only used one ticket each the whole week as no-one ever took the tickets. It was an adventure.

It wasn't until 1981 when we made it back to the north. We had an old Hillman Imp and a new Cabanon tent. The car overheated on hills which is not a good idea when going over Slochd Summit on the A9 or the road from Lochcarron to Kyle of Lochalsh. We got as far as Gairloch with the aim of retracing my childhood holiday memories and then travelled down through Torridon to Kyle of Lochalsh. We crossed on the ferry over to Skye and drove round much of the island on an extremely wet evening, not seeing a thing because of the continuous downpour. We crossed back over to Kyle and in desperation somehow found a campsite sign at 11 pm and pitched the tent in the dark. We woke up the next morning in a bare field with a huge host of midges. We beat a hasty retreat down to Fort William.

Camping in Glen Nevis, 1981

We returned to Gairloch the following year with a red Ford Escort (the Imp had to be put down). We had a day trip to Ullapool and the wonders of Assynt and also discovered Mellon Udrigle. Again we went down to Skye but this time conditions were kind and we camped overnight and then to our favourite Glen Nevis campsite at Fort William.

During the next few years we were distracted by the lure of the Mediterranean beach holiday. When I started painting in 1987 my subject matter was mainly local to the Currie and Balerno area outside Edinburgh where we stayed. We did have a brief first visit to Mull at a B&B in Dervaig, including an inspiring day out to Iona, and I produced a handful of small paintings from that trip. In 1990 we tried camping again and returned to Gairloch but in an even smaller tent. Unfortunately there was a plague of midges one morning and our tent was literally covered in them (don't get a dark green tent). There were even midges in the shower. We escaped to the Ceilidh Place bunk house in Ullapool. My paintings were still predominantly local at this time but I was now producing more and also larger paintings from our northern trips.

Then of course we moved to Clovenfords in 1991 and there was little money available for trips away. Mary's younger brother died later that year. In 1993 Mary had to undergo surgery. To aid her recovery we rented a rather clunky campervan for a week and headed up north, staying at Pitlochry and then on to Ullapool. We drove out the single track road to Achiltibuie and stayed at Achnahaird campsite. It was one of the more basic campsites in Scotland with one cold tap though it did have a toilet block. But it was also one of the most spectacular sitting as it did in the dunes above Achnahaird beach. It also had an almost surreal view of the mountains of Assynt as they pop up spread across the horizon. It unfortunately closed down a year or two later. We had travelled through Assynt previously but had been unaware of the short road to Achiltibuie and the Summer Isles and this was a great discovery for us. We were to return many times in later years. Our tour continued down to Kyle of Lochalsh, across to Skye and Armadale and the ferry to Mallaig. This was to become one of our favourite southward routes.

This campervan tour was perhaps the real beginning of our journeys to the west coast and its integral relationship with my work. Thereafter we began to rent cottages and made trips every year – to Mull, Islay, Ullapool, the Summer Isles and Ardnamurchan. We ventured out to Harris in 1999 and then again in 2004. We developed a love for the islands. It is quite a magical experience to arrive at an island by Cal Mac ferry as you then enter a different world with every island offering its own unique experience. Tiree, Colonsay, Orkney (a return), South Uist (including Eriskay and Barra) and North Uist followed over the years.

In 2007 we rented another campervan, this time a bit more modern, which enabled us to travel up to Durness. This is one of my favourite campsites sitting on the cliff overlooking Sango Bay, as well as being close to the amazing Balnakeil Beach. We travelled down via Ullapool and Gairloch to Kyle of Lochalsh, Armadale and ferry to Mallaig, staying overnight at Camusdarach

Our cottage at Meavag, Isle of Harris, 2004

Tiree, 2005

Rented campervan at Ullapool campsite, 2007

Loch Assynt, 2007

View of Hoy from our cottage near Stromness, Orkney, 2006

Colonsay, 2008

Near Duart Castle, Mull, 2009

Ullapool, 2009

Bongo, Durness, 2010

Bongo, Sunnyside Croft, Bunacaimbe, 2012

campsite. We awoke very early to find the weather changing and we made a quick decision to go to Iona! We left about 6 or 7 am, drove to Acharacle and Strontian, down through Morvern and then to the ferry at Lochaline. It was a Sunday morning and I recall we didn't see another vehicle till we reached the ferry. We crossed over to Fishnish on Mull and then to Fionnphort and Fidden Farm campsite. We went over on to Iona for the afternoon. Certainly the most memorable drive we ever did.

In 2009 we tried camping again – bigger tent – but the midges besieged us in Glen Nevis campsite on a very warm and clammy uncomfortable evening. I had been looking at campervans for a few years in a fairly obsessive way and in 2010 we took the plunge and bought a Mazda Bongo. Bongos are imported from Japan and though quite old (a 1998 in our case) are much cheaper than UK campers. We had it converted to our spec as a high top and we were off, with the addition of a stand alone, drive away awning. The van had a V6 petrol engine and was lovely to drive though it guzzled petrol. We didn't have much space and the van was crammed full of our stuff. We slept in the van but set up kitchen in the awning with a large dometic fridge and even a small electric oven. It was a home from home though a great deal of work setting up and dismantling camp. We did get some puzzled looks from caravanners and motorhomers, but aspirational glances from young tenters. However, the advantage of a Bongo is that it can go anywhere.

After three years in the Bongo, much as we had really enjoyed it, we had had enough of the effort involved and returned to renting cottages. In turn, after a while we once again became frustrated with cottage life: the advance booking, the commitment to a particular week and lack of flexibility, and the long drives to get there.

It's a puzzle trying to see the best of Scotland. From the artist's point of view cottages are probably best. They let you stay and absorb one place for a time. If you do as I do and take lots of photographs, you can learn about the area and watch the weather. You are ready when circumstances are right. But personally I do feel hemmed in and you are still living

A rented static caravan at Bunacaimbe near Arisaig, 2014

Our Hymer caravan at Ullapool, 2017

in someone else's house. Probably the real way to tour Scotland is in a campervan or motorhome. They can, however, be ridiculously expensive to buy or rent, but they do allow flexibility and freedom to explore the country and respond to the weather. But they also create the problem that for any excursion, your whole home has to go with you. Camping is certainly the cheapest, but at a certain age the lack of basic comforts, as well as exposure to the midge, are off-putting. And so, in our case, the touring caravan gradually evolved as the obvious solution.

It had always made perfect sense: more space and comfort than a campervan and a bigger bed. But there was always the intimidating prospect of towing and difficulty going on narrow roads. In 2015 an opportunity presented itself and we bought a small Hymer Feeling 230 at a very good price. We found the towing to be nowhere near as difficult as imagined, though reversing can be perplexing, and embarrassing! Our caravan is very small, easily towable with an ordinary family car, and still feels like camping. This will be us for a long time I would hope.

I do love campsites. Life is good in the fresh air. Campsites can be interesting in their diversity and a range of people can be met. In

Ullapool we once pitched between a £60,000 motorhome on one side, and Dave from Pickering on the other. Dave was in an old panel van with no windows (cost him £200) and just a mattress in the back. He was a big chap, wore shorts (not always a t-shirt or top) and flip-flops regardless of the weather and often had a can of lager in hand. He and his wife had been married at Clashnessie Beach near Clachtoll a few years before and had a remarkable knowledge of Scotland. They were not what they first appeared. The further north one travels the more noticeable the range of people met, including many Dutch and Germans. There are more large expensive motorhomes and caravans these days but one still sees the strange and unique. People find their own solutions, both economically and practically, to the task of touring the north west. Speaking to people it becomes clear that others are trying to find what's right for them, whether tent, trailer tent, small camper, large motorhome or caravan. We have seen small VW vans with young families crammed in the windowless back, landrovers with tents on the roof, and even a panel van with a motorcycle kept in the back beside the bed.

Flat Eric, our caravan travelling companion, relaxing at Bunacaimbe, 2016

Loch nan Uamh   40 x 40 cm   2015
On the road from Fort William to Mallaig.

Winter Crows 90 x 110 cm   2012

Clovenfords, Scottish Borders

Mary and I have lived in our cottage overlooking Clovenfords for over 25 years. Clovenfords is a small village a short distance from the amenities of Galashiels. We are only an hour from Edinburgh by car or by the relatively new train from Galashiels. It's a very easy place to live: lovely scenery, decent facilities, very good healthcare, friendly people, quiet roads and nothing is far away.

When I first moved here I had trouble adjusting to translating the new scenery into paint. When the snow arrived all was transformed. I have had no need to venture far from our house for painting material and have not progressed to painting the Borders countryside apart from a handful of pictures of the Eildons. Every subject has been within walking distance. I gradually began to understand the surrounding

Snow on Craig Hill above Clovenfords
Our cottage can just be seen on the right at the foot of the hill.

Borders Snow   100 x 130 cm   2012
Just above Clovenfords on Craig Hill. The Yair Hill can be seen in the backgound, a regular feature in my local paintings.

landscape with its dykes, old gates, sheep and groups of trees. We do get marvellous skies here. I continue to paint mainly snow scenes though there have been fewer falls in recent winters. There seems to be a similarity between snow and the sea, due to the moisture in the air and interactions with sunlight.

Around 1750 Clovenfords Inn was a staging post for the mail coach from Edinburgh to Carlisle. Sir Walter Scott stayed at the inn before moving to nearby Ashiestiel House. His statue outside the present hotel was made by a Galashiels painter and decorator and was erected in 1911. The village was famous for a thriving vinery for over 90 years, started in 1869. Its Muscat grapes were despatched by train from the village station even to Harrods in London. Sadly, when we arrived in Clovenfords only one run down greenhouse remained. There is now a group of houses on its site.

When we moved to Clovenfords in 1991, the village was a mix of "old Cloven" and "new Cloven" with a contingent of strong country characters. The day we moved in within half an hour we were greeted over the front gate by an elderly gentleman wearing a cattle coat and bunnet, with his shepherd's stick and Border Terrier, requesting "An' whit dae you dae fur a crust?" This was Scotty Elliot and his dog Gatsby (never on a lead), a retired farmer who lived just down the road from us. His wife Phemie (Euphemia) was larger than life. At a later date when I helped with their new video player I was gifted two large leeks.

We were also fortunate when we first arrived to befriend Archie, a dyker and former shepherd who spent most of his time in the countryside around Clovenfords. He had worked for Scotty as a shepherd and they were quite a pair together. Archie liked a dram, and the ladies, and always had a joke to tell, usually about an Irishman. He had an intimate knowledge of the local area and organised the local pheasant shoot with a group of assorted locals and friends, based in "Archie's shed" beside our old garage. His favourite pastime was to sit in a field with his dog Tess hoping to shoot a few pigeons or "vermin" as he described them.

I am not a fan of shooting, and probably dislike it even more now, but that was his way and we learned much from Archie. He would drop by on a regular basis since he was always passing in his old Subaru pick-up. He loved to see the local paintings and was quite perplexed if he couldn't recognise the exact location.

Times have changed and Clovenfords, though larger now, is a quieter place. There are more new houses and cars are bigger and more expensive than they were. Many of the country characters have sadly passed on. It is an easier existence somehow: facilities in nearby Galashiels are much better while our lives have become simpler and quieter. Apart from regular trips to Edinburgh only our forays up north take us further away. But we are always happy to return. We will be here in Clovenfords for some time I imagine.

May, the Eildons oil on board 68 x 90 cm 2005
An early picture of that well known Borders landmark, but seen from the road past Gattonside.

Newhall   80 x 120 cm   2011

The three way road junction at Newhall Farm, the traditional home of the Elliots, a well known local farming family (not related to Scotty Elliot). Cauld Face is the hill on the left above Laidlawstiel Farm. This is a regular walk for Mary and I up to the wee "humpy bridge", just out of picture on the left, over the Caddon Water.

January Track 80 x 120 cm 2017
The track to Torwoodlee, looking back towards Clovenfords with the Yair Hill on the left.

Stubble Field: Rooks and Crows   60 x 90 cm   2015

We see great skies to the south and east from our house. This is south to the Yair Hill seen from our back door.

Tracks to Torwoodlee   120 x 150 cm   2009

Further along the track to Torwoodlee. The farm can be seen while Torwoodlee House, the home of the Pringles the lairds of Galashiels, is beyond in the woods.

Track down the Hll   80 x 100 cm   2015

This is the track above Old Redhead cottage leading up to 13th century Whytbank Tower which was restored in the early 90s. Our friend Archie worked on many of the old garden walls in the restoration. Beyond can be seen the Caddon Valley.

January Day   90 x 110 cm   2009

This shows the corner of our back garden with Whytbank Farm at the top of the hill. Sadly the farm was sold and transformed into a group of rental cottages as well as a riding stable – though I must say when the horses are ridden in the field it makes a lovely sight.

Home & Studio, Winter 40 x 40 cm 2009
Bowland Road leading up from the village to
our house.

New Lamb mixed media 40 x 40 cm
2007
The old barn at Whytbank Farm featured
in several paintings but was alas knocked
down some years ago. The ewe and lamb are
Suffolks, my favourite breed.

Field mixed media 20 x 22 cm 2014
The field directly behind our house looking
up to Whytbank.

Snow Road 30 x 30 cm 2011
This is the road going past the side of our house up to
Whytbank Farm, on to Newhall and eventually to Stow. My
framing workshop is seen on the right.

Hawthorn 30 x 40 cm 2012

Farm Track, Whytbank   oil on board   40 x 46 cm   2003

Silver Tweed   oil on board   60 x 71 cm   2004
A view of the River Tweed from below Laidlawstiel House.

Winter Valley   20 x 50 cm   2011
Our regular local walk along the road up the Caddon Valley to Newhall Farm.

Winter Morning   90 x 110 cm   2009
The morning sun appearing behind Meigle Hill as seen from my studio. The village of Clovenfords is just down the hill.

Storm Approaching   72 x 93 cm   2016
Bunacaimbe beach with a threatening cloud obscuring Eigg and Rum.

Arisaig to Mallaig

It seems appropriate that the first north west trip Mary and I undertook together was to Arisaig in 1975. At the time we picked a rental cottage purely by chance from an advert in The Scotsman. We had no idea of where we were going. How did one do these things pre-internet?

Nowadays, along with Fort William, this is our comfort zone. This is where we go to just be for a few days. With the campervan and now the caravan it's an easy drive to Fort William. There we can escape and relax into the campsite lifestyle. Next morning its just a short trip to Arisaig. Though it can be said about much of the west coast, there is nowhere quite like that short stretch of coast from Arisaig to Mallaig. The dominating presence of Eigg and Rum on the horizon is quite stunning. The changes in light as the day progresses are particularly noticeable here: a soft gentle light in the morning and later, as the sun comes round past Ardnamurchan to the south, those spectacular late afternoons, evenings and sunsets.

Camusdarach beach

Apart from that first basic cottage we've stayed there in a log cabin, a couple of residential caravans, tents, rented campervans, Bongo and now the caravan. We once rented a cottage positioned directly on Camusdarach beach. It wasn't luxury accommodation but what a location. It was a particularly good week because of the exceptionally hot and sunny weather even though it was only mid April. The beaches have also been a good day excursion when staying in Fort William.

We've been there at various times of the year from April to October and the evenings can be so different with the sun going down from behind the Sgurr of Eigg and up to the north of Rum and nearing Skye. I have regularly been down on the beach in those evenings and it can be bitterly cold off season. It is not necessarily a hugely active place, and days can be spent simply with perhaps a short trip to Mallaig and walks on the beaches. There are bigger walks of course and kayaking is very popular. The Mallaig ferry offers opportunities for day trips to Skye or perhaps to Plockton. There are also sails to the Small Isles – Muck, Eigg, Rum and Canna – and also Loch Nevis. On bad weather days Fort William is only an hour away. There is usually a breeze and so not much midge activity. It is a place to do not very much and bask in the views of Eigg and Rum from Bunacaimbe, Traigh, Camusdarach and Morar beaches.

Calm Sea, Traigh   oil on board   30 x 90 cm   2005

Evening Sea   80 x 100 cm   2014
A spectacular evening on Camusdarach beach in April looking on to Rum.

Dog Walkers, West Coast   70 x 100 cm   2015
Late afternoon on Bunacaimbe beach. Sunnyside Croft campsite has a gate directly on to the beach.

Bunacaimbe   100 x 130 cm   2012

This is from the track down to Bunacaimbe beach from Sunnyside Croft. There is another older campsite just to the right. This stretch of coastline has several other campsites which people regularly frequent year after year. Sunnyside Croft is a more recent addition which is reflected in its very modern facilities.

Evening Clouds, Eigg & Rum   51 x 76 cm   2015

The evenings are quite unpredictable. A beautiful day might just fade quietly away while a dark, cloudy day might just burst into spectacular life as the sun lowers in the sky.

K24   oil on board   76 x 81 cm   2000

K24 sat on Traigh beach at an old boatshed. The painting was exhibited at my first Dundas Street Gallery. A lady had come into the show and was interested in a small painting and then came back with her husband, a retired seaman, who duly purchased this much bigger picture instead. They later took a trip to see the boat.

West Coast Cat mixed media 15 x 24 cm 2013
The resident cat at Sunnyside Croft campsite, Bunnacaimbe.

West Coast, Passing Gull mixed media 15 x 24 cm 2013

West Coast Gate 40 x 60 cm 2015
I have painted three different pictures of this lovely old gate. It's to the south of the Camusdarach beaches. I've always had an interest in painting gates, often leading on to beaches or views, in this case Eigg & Rum.

Traigh Morning   72 x 93 cm   2016

Traigh beach is a small bay or cove and sits in front of the famous Traigh golf course, the most westerly course on the UK mainland (9 holes, par 68). This is from the south side looking to Sleat and the Cuillins.

Traigh means beach in Gaelic and is seen in many location names thoughout the north west and islands.

Two Beaches   70 x 100 cm   2016

If the tide is out on Camusdarach it is possible to walk directly to the next beach where a line of dunes point toward Eigg and Rum. There is another idylic little beach on the south side of the dunes which is depicted on the opposite page (bottom).

Dark Wave
40 x 60 cm   2016
A calm day on
Camusdarach beach
looking across to Skye,
the Sleat Peninsula and
the Cuillins.

Crossing the Beach
30 x 40 cm   2016

Iona Light 80 x 100 cm 2016

Iona & Mull

We have stayed in various parts of Mull but have found the Craignure area to be the most convenient location for getting around the island, as well as being the ferry terminal. The castles at Torosay and Duart are nearby and picturesque Tobermory is an easy drive. Loch na Keal, the island of Ulva and the road up the west coast (very winding and slow with some unexpected steep hills and bends) to Calgary Bay are easily accessible. I love the drive through Glen More, very open and quite quick though single track, and then it slows down along the Ross of Mull to Fionnphort and Iona.

Iona is always like a magnet for us when we are on Mull. One year we had a week in Fionnphort with various destinations in mind, but ended up just crossing over to Iona every day. We did face the usual problem in Scotland, namely the weather. It was a pretty good dry week but there were only two days with good light. From my perspective those flat

Crossing the machair
towards the North End
on Iona, 2016

Firth of Lorn   60 x 80 cm   2017
Looking south between the Isle of Kerrera and Mull.

lightless days sometimes encountered are just not very good. Mull can be extremely wet, but even on cloudy, rainy days the light can suddenly change. There is always a chance of better weather in the far west, particularly on the Ross of Mull towards Iona.

The quirkiest accommodation we had was at Killunaig overlooking Loch Scridain. I had been offered a week at a converted church in exchange for me creating a small painting of the area. On approach it looked quite impressive but inside it was very quirky and Heath Robinson. The ex-church windows were high up which restricted any view. The bathroom had antique fittings from a London hotel while the electrics were quite bewildering.

Iona north beach might well be the most magical place in Scotland. It certainly has a spiritual quality all of its own quite separate from the island's religious history. Anyone encountered on the beach is courteously friendly but tends to keep their own mesmerised peaceful space. It does have a remarkable combination of features: the startling white sand, the dark rocks, the incredible colour of the sea, the spit of sand (tombolo) on Storm Island, and the dramatic presence of the cliffs of the Burg on Mull with Ben More behind. Clouds tend to be drawn in by Ben More resulting in a steady line of clouds over Mull while keeping Iona relatively cloud free. The beach also faces north which results in an unusual consistency of light, without the dramatic changes seen in westerly aspects such as Arisaig.

North Beach Waves
20 x 50 cm   2011

Dozing Sheep, Iona 40 x 40 cm 2015

Iona Farm 50 x 60 cm 2014
Ardiona Croft, looking north to Mull.

Iona is well known as a favourite location for painters and particularly its connection with the Scottish Colourists. A fascinating book by Philip MacLeod Coupe (*Paintings of Iona: Peploe and Cadell*) describes paintings and locations around the island. It also notes the reduced levels of sand at the north end. I checked my own photographs and was amazed to see the dramatic reduction in areas of sand since I first went to Iona. This was especially noticeable on the east side at Strand of the Monks.

I haven't produced as many paintings on Mull itself though Loch na Keal has always been of interest to me. It's just a case of being there when the light is suitable. Loch na Keal is also a good place to possibly spot sea eagles and otters. Strangely my best sightings of the latter have been once at Craignure while waiting on the ferry as an otter basked on its back very close to the shore. The other occasion was seeing a very relaxed otter in Tobermory harbour while it used an RNLI dinghy as

North Shore, Iona   51 x 76 cm   2015
Storm Island is on the left and Mull in the distance, with a glimpse of the beach of the North End.

a base to catch fish. Wildlife tends to be seen when least expected. At a couple of places we have stayed on Mull sea eagles were a daily sight – no travelling involved. Last year one soared high above the ferry as it sailed back to Oban.

As well as its scenery, Mull has a great range of attractions for the visitor including wildlife, walking and sails to the Treshnish Isles. The short ferry crossing from Tobermory across to Kilchoan on Ardnamurchan gives easy access to Sanna Beach if you take your car.

Rocks & Grasses, Iona   60 x 80 cm   2014
Cow's Rock at the North End. On Mull, from the left, the entrance to Loch na Keal, the cliffs of Gribun, Ben More and the Burg, Ben Buie and Loch Scridain and then the Ross of Mull.

Iona North End   80 x 100 cm   2015
The rocks known as The Finger in the centre and Cow's Rock on the right of the north beach, with Storm Island, Mull and the Ross of Mull.

Iona Summer (The Finger)   51 x 76 cm   2014

After the Storm   80 x 120 cm   2010

Hens & Washing, Iona   mixed media   15 x 15 cm   2014

Shorn Tups, Iona   mixed media   13 x 14 cm   2009
The road to the North End, looking back towards the Abbey and village.

An island Scene   30 x 40 cm   2014
Loooking over Lagandorain croft, the Dutchman's Cap on the horizon.

West Coast, Mull   90 x 110 cm   2010
Overlooking Loch na Keal with the island of Eorsa, the cliffs of Ardmeanach and the island of Inch Kenneth, onetime home of the Mitfords, further out. The island of Ulva is just out of picture on the right.

Eorsa, Loch na Keal   60 x 90 cm   2014

Loch Scridain   40 x 40 cm   2014

The road west from Craignure descends out of Glen More to Loch Scridain. There is a turn off to the right up over to Loch na Keal, otherwise the road continues to Pennyghael, Bunessan and the ferrry to Iona at Fionnphort.

Passing Duart   80 x 100   2017

The ferry from Oban to Mull is perhaps my favourite crossing – great scenery south through the Firth of Lorn, north up to Ben Nevis and also the gradually increasing presence of Mull and Ben More. A significant feature of the crossing is Duart Castle sitting on its rocky promontory near Craignure. Originally built in the 13th century, it fell into ruin but was restored at the beginning of the 20th century. It is the seat of the Clan MacLean.

Trees & Castle, Mull   40 x 80 cm   2010

The Lighthouse   40 x 50 cm   2017
The lighthouse near Tobermory.

Gannet 20 x 20 cm 2010

I do love gannets. A memorable
sighting was at the far end of
Luskentyre on Harris when we
watched a solitary bird put on a
soaring and diving display, not a
soul in sight.

Islands

As well as some magnificent scenery, unpredictable weather and ferocious midges, Scotland also has a grand collection of islands around its coast, from Ailsa Craig in the south west, up to the Shetland Isles in the far north, and then the Isle of May and Bass Rock in the south east. There are hundreds of islands of all sorts and sizes – small skerries up to the largest, the Isle of Lewis.

I do love islands. As I said previously, there is a certain magic as an island is approached on a Cal Mac ferry. There is the pleasure of discovering an island's unique character. There is a sadness too when one leaves and it can be quite a shock arriving back in "civilisation". Drivers can be in such a hurry when they disembark and quickly revert to mainland characteristics. I usually pull over quite early and let them all pass. I found it particularly noticeable at Uig on Skye when coming back from

The south east corner of Colonsay, with the Paps of Jura beyond, 2008

Harris or North Uist. Rush, rush, rush. It doesn't take long for that more relaxed attitude of the islands to dissipate. I always prefer to ease the transition with an overnight stay somewhere en route.

We have stayed on quite a few islands, while making day excursions to Gigha, Jura, Muck, Barra and Lewis. Islands such as Staffa and Handa are only accessible for the day anyway but are well worth it. There are still islands I want to explore as well as others I cannot see myself going to. I am not a brave enough sailor to try for St Kilda!

We went twice to Islay in the mid 90s. The "Queen of the Hebrides" is a very different island in that much of it is agricultural and well known for its dairy produce. I remember being taken aback when many of the local drivers gave a friendly wave when passing by. I particularly liked its west

Paps of Jura from Ghia
oil on board
40 x 46 cm   2004

coast which was much more Hebridean in feel – Machir Bay and Saligo Bay come to mind. Gruinart Bay was a favourite with lovely beaches and views of the Paps of Jura. It is also an RSPB reserve. The island is known for its wide range of bird life including some 50,000 migrating geese over the winter. It is famous historically for Finlaggan Loch, the seat of the Lords of the Isles in the 13th to 15th centuries, and also Kildalton Cross, one of the finest early Christian crosses in Scotland. Of course, if you like whisky there are several distilleries.

Our first trip to Harris was in 1999 when we stayed in a cottage on Luskentyre. The cottage looked fine in its leaflet but in reality left much to be desired. We suspected that a previous occupant had used some wooden slats from the bed as firewood! We returned to Harris in 2004 having been invited by Ian Scarr-Hall of Amhuinnsuidhe Castle after he had purchased one of my paintings at Panter & Hall. We stayed in his family's old holiday cottage at Meavag on the east side of Harris. He very kindly gave Mary and I a personal tour of the castle and we saw his collection of fine paintings. The west coast beaches on Harris –

The Cottage at Meavag oil on board 30 x 80 cm 2005

Balephuil, Tiree   90 x 120 cm   2005

A charming hamlet of cottages overlooks beautiful Balephuil Bay in the south east of the island. Traditional housing on the "sunshine isle" consists of two main types: the white house and the pudding (or spotted) house, the latter indigenous to the island. Modern architect designed versions of these traditional styles can also be seen on the island.

Skerryvore Lighthouse, designed by Alan Stevenson and built between 1838 and 1844, can be seen on clear days from the bay on the horizon approximately ten miles south.

Luskentyre, Seilebost, Horgabost, Scarista and Huishnish – have to be seen to be believed. The east coast is completely different consisting of rocky inlets connected by "The Golden Road". At the south end of the island Rodel Church is well worth a visit.

I was very excited to go to Tiree in 2005. It had such romantic connotations plus all those famous beaches. It is reputedly the sunniest place in Scotland. Our cottage looked great from the outside sitting amidst the bright green machair. Inside it was a sad disappointment and we had to spend a deal of time cleaning it to a reasonable level. The bedroom was fairly creepy and we ended up sleeping on the lounge floor. It was tempting to leave but we stuck it out. Tiree is a beautiful place but for some reason it just did not click with us and I found it quite tricky to extract painting material. I did like Balephuil and Coalas though and got half a dozen nice paintings from the trip. I also made a series of small pictures of old post boxes which I found of interest.

In 2006 we returned to Orkney. We revisited the same sites as in 1975: Skara Brae, Maeshowe, Ring of Brodgar and a few more. Our cottage, a couple of miles outside Stromness, had a great view of Hoy. Orkney has its own charms but is so different from the islands in the west. It feels very orderly, the roads are excellent and the landscape quite gentle. Birsay was a remarkable island accessed on foot via a causeway. The cliffs at the bird reserve of Marwick Head were especially spectacular (and very intimidating), described as a "seabird city" by the RSPB. We paid a nostalgic trip to Stromness campsite and while standing on the old pier saw a huge basking shark swim by just a few yards away. We also visited an old acquaintance now married to a local farmer and we were amazed to discover how the Orcadians were so well travelled, thinking nothing of going off anywhere in the UK or the world despite the additional travel involved from Orkney. They also took us on their old fishing boat from Kirkwall to the uninhabited island of Gairsay where they kept some sheep. While they attended to their sheep Mary and I walked over to a bay on the other side of the island where we encountered some very inquisitive seals – a lovely and quite eery experience.

Skara Brae, Orkney, 2006

Curious seals, Gairsay, 2006

Colonsay beckoned in 2008 and we stayed at Lower Kilchattan, near the unique Colonsay Bookshop. Kiloran Bay is well known and there is good walk beyond which leads to Balnahard Bay looking across to Mull. I found the south east corner of the island of most interest and also the walk at low tide across the Strand to Oronsay with its marvellous beaches and views to Jura. I do remember the weather was remarkably hot and sunny all week which was exceptional for May.

In 2010 we bought our Mazda Bongo campervan and our first trip was up through Skye and across to a campsite on Benbecula for a couple of nights. We had a great third night wild camping on Berneray beside the beach on the north east side. The weather wasn't great but when we returned to Skye the sun came out and we stayed at Uig for a few days. Skye is a great favourite with many people and so that was a good opportunity for us to see a bit more of the island.

2012 was a very poor summer and in desperation we booked a last minute cottage in South Uist, though we travelled in the Bongo which was great for overnight stays en route. The cottage was lovely and we

Wild camping on Berneray, 2010

South Uist, 2011

were right on a beach but somehow I couldn't find too much of interest for painting. We did take the opportunity to drive down to Eriskay, which I really liked, and then across to Barra for the day.

On a drive through North Uist to Berneray we found this more appealing and so the following year we rented a cottage at Sollas. I loved the dunes and beaches in the north west corner. It had a lovely wildness and we would often have a beach all to ourselves. It wasn't particularly successful as a painting trip due to a lack of good light that week but we just felt very comfortable there, though it was always very windy!

It can seem a long journey to get to many of the islands, often involving an overnight stay en route. Perhaps that adds to the mystique, that other worldliness. We have always been quite lucky with the weather in terms of not too much rain. What we did experience on the Uists, apart from incessant wind, was a strangely diffused light even on days where the sky seemed quite clear and blue. We didn't see dramatic clouds or weather changes which I rather like for my work. I don't know how common this feature of the light might be or perhaps it was the time of year.

Corner of the Garden, Colonsay   50 x 60 cm   2009
Looking south from the garden of the cottage where we stayed at Kilchattan on Colonsay.

Kiloran Wave   70 x 80 cm   2009
Kiloran Bay is a well known attraction on Colonsay.

Colonsay Hens   70 x 80 cm   2009

The yard of one of a group of cottages overlooking Kiloran Bay on Colonsay.

Summer Cliffs, Skye   70 x 100 cm   2011

The cliffs south of the spectacular Mealt Waterfall and Kilt Rock on the north east coast of Skye.

Big Rum, Little Canna
30 x 60 cm   2014
As seen from the north
coast of Sleat, Skye.

Leaving Barra
50 x 50 cm   2014

Seilebost & Luskentyre   60 x 90 cm   2005

Seilebost in the foreground looking on to Luskentyre and the Hills of Harris. Taransay can just be glimpsed on the left.

Distant Harris   20 x 76 cm   2014
The hills of Harris seen across Traigh Ear, North Uist.

North Uist Grasses   30 x 60 cm   2014
Looking across Traigh Ear from Machair Leathann, North Uist.

Corran Aird a' Mhorain, North Uist   80 x 120 cm   2012

This is a remarkable feature where a thin line of dunes and sand stretch into the sea back towards the small island of Orasay and the hills of North Uist. It is accessed from Grenitote (Greinetobht) and a walk across Traigh Ear.

Gentle Light, Berneray   50 x 50 cm   2014

Berneray Dune   40 x 40 cm   2011

Hoy, from Outertown   oil on board   35 x 38 cm   2007

Isle of May
30 x 60 cm   2015

Bass Rock, Belhaven
20 x 50 cm   2015

Islands of the East
30 x 60 cm   2014
Bass Rock and Isle of
May

Badentarbat Shore   40 x 40 cm   2011

Achiltibuie & the Summer Isles

Achiltibuie should theoretically feature in the next section on the north west but it has played such a big part in my work. We have stayed there several times and had day trips while staying in Ullapool. I made it the main feature of my exhibition at Bourne Fine Art in 2011.

Achiltibuie feels like an island. The twisting passing place road through Assynt, past Cul Beg and Stac Pollaidh, has been much improved in recent years, and though not really far, can feel as though one might never get to the end. Watch out for the delivery drivers and locals who are well used to the road. The area generates a feeling of peaceful isolation and days can be whiled away doing not very much.

Looking out over Tanera Mor and the rest of the Summer Isles, 2008

Ahiltibuie is on the Coigach peninsula. The area consists of a short stretch of coastline from Reiff in the north through Altandhu, Dornie, Polbain, Badentarbat, Achiltibuie village, Polglass and Badenscallie to Culnacraig at the south end. Looking out to sea an assortment of islands can be seen including Isle Ristoll, Tanera Beag, Tanera Mor and Horse Island, collectively known as the Summer Isles. There is also a beautiful beach at Achnahaird with spectacular views to the mountains of Assynt: Canisp, Quinag, Suilven, Cul Mor, Cul Beg, Stac Pollaidh and Ben Mor Coigach.

There is a very good boat trip from Ullapool which goes round the islands. There is also a smaller local boat tour from Badentarbat which is well worth doing.

James Morrison has been painting the area regularly since the late 1980s and I have always admired his grand depictions of Suilven with towering clouds above. Will Maclean, the highly regarded Scottish artist known for his meaningful boxes and constructions, has close links with Achiltibuie as his father was brought up in Polbain. I have seen works and drawings based on the area by him as well as his painter wife Marian Leven. I was surprised when I came across the English artist Peter Coker's (1926–2004) sketches and paintings of Achiltibuie and the Summer Isles from his visits there in the late 1980s.

An excellent book *Island Farm* by Frank Fraser Darling describes his years (1938 to 1944) on Tanera Mor, the largest of the islands. His earlier book *Island Years*, about his times on the Treshnish Isles and then the very remote North Rona, is equally fascinating.

Towards Ben Mor Coigach
46 x 55 cm   2011
Brooding Ben Mor Coigach looms above the line of houses of Achiltibuie village, Polglass and Badenscallie, while Loch Broom stretches in the distance beyond Horse Island south east to Ullapool.

Achiltibuie Panorama   30 x 120 cm   2011
An unusual painting in that it encompasses an extremely wide angle vista well over 180° from the mountains of Assynt on the left to Tanera Mor and Tanera Beag on the right. The villages can just be seen along the coastline with Horse Island in the centre of the picture. There is actually a very small dot in the bay at Tanera Mor to indicate the *Hebridean Princess* which was anchored there.

Summer Isles   50 x 100 cm   2011

Overlooking Horse island   50 x 100 cm   2011

Badentarbat Bay   50 x 100 cm   2011

Beyond Altandhu   50 x 100 cm   2011

Wet Sands, Achnahaird   50 x 100 cm   2011

Achnahaird Bay   30 x 60 cm   2011

Achnahaird Dunes   73 x 92 cm   2017

Achiltibuie   30 x 40 cm   2012

Tanera Mor from Badenscallie   30 x 40 cm   2002

Distant Mountains, Summer isles   40 x 80 cm   2012

Assynt   30 x 40 cm   2011
The single track road from the coast at Altandhu across the moor to Achnahaird and magnificent views to the mountains of Assynt.

Oldshoremore Waves 46 x 55 cm 2010

North West

Ardnamurchan lies north of Mull and south of Arisaig. Ardnamurchan Point, with its lighthouse designed by Alan Stevenson, is the most westerly point on the British mainland. Ardnamurchan has been described as a punctuation mark separating the north and south Hebridean seas, reflected by the prevalence for Irish and Scots influence to the south and Scandinavian Norse to the north.*

In common with Achiltibuie, Ardnamurchan can often feel like an island. Access is by a short crossing on the Corran Ferry near Onich. The road fairly soon becomes restricted to passing places and is slow and twisting through the woods along the shore of Loch Sunart. Journey time is much longer than the distance would suggest. The landscape opens up just after Glenborrodale and the road climbs up behind Ben Hiant to reveal views of Rum and Eigg to the north. It can be confusing as the

* *The Hebrides: an aerial view of a cultural landscape* by Angus & Patricia Macdonald

Ullapool, 2015
The new Stornoway ferry (*MV Loch Seaforth*) and a cruise ship on Loch Broom.

islands have reverse positions from the customary view from Arisaig. We had a beautiful week on the northern coast at Achateny in April 2000. I think I had "view overload" by the end of the week!

Red deer on the hills are a common sight here as the road turns back down to the south towards Kilchoan where there is the small ferry to Tobermory on Mull. There is now the option of going either to Ardnamurchan Point as well as Portuairk, or directly to Sanna Bay. We had a week at Portuairk in 2001 from which I produced all the paintings for a solo exhibition stand at ArtLondon with Ainscough Contemporary Art. Sanna Bay is considered by some to be the most beautiful beach in Scotland. There is a car park at Sanna which gives no hint of the beach's presence. I did once see someone drive up and park, get out for a quick survey, and then leave in apparent disappointment. There are assorted cottages scattered over the open grassland, including some very new architect designed ones. Just over the dunes lies the stunning beach. There is a very good walk over the hill to Portuairk.

Alasdair Maclean's *Night Falls on Ardnamurchan* gives a fascinating account of croft life at Sanna in the 1960s and 70s.

Portuairk from Sanna   40 x 80 cm   2005
Looking south from Sanna to Portuairk. Ardnamurchan Point is on the extreme right with the lighthouse just out of sight.

Sanna View   60 x 90 cm   2005

This is from the south on the walk across the hill to Portuairk. The small island of Muck can be seen just in front of Rum with Eigg to the right and then Skye in the distance. The cottages of Sanna are on the machair above the beach.

Big Cloud over Portuairk   90 x 110 cm   2017

Returning to Salen the road north passes through Acharacle and Moidart to join up with the Fort William to Mallaig road. By crossing on the ferry from Mallaig to Armadale on Skye the road can be taken through the Sleat Peninsula and across the Skye Bridge to Kyle of Lochalsh. Nearby is the picture postcard village of Plockton. The road winds north by beautiful Locharron and offers the opportunity to branch off to Applecross via the infamous Pass of the Cattle. Otherwise it heads up through the mountains of Torridon to Kinlochewe. Alternatively the easier road can be taken to Achnasheen and then west to Kinlochewe. Both these routes have been very familiar to me but always in the reverse direction when journeying south from Ullapool or Gairloch. With the caravan the passing place roads are now unfortunately something I prefer to avoid. From Kinlochewe, Loch Maree is a beautiful drive with Slioch dominating above. Gairloch is a lovely village and there is a very good campsite in the dunes at Big Sands though it does get very busy in the season with holidaymakers.

Plockton Bay
oil on board
60 x 80 cm   2002

Walker & Dog   80 x 100 cm   2012
The beach at Big Sands, Gairloch, looking across to Skye.

Beach Stream, Mellon Udrigle 80 x 120 cm   2007
A beautiful beach with stunning views across to Achiltibuie and Assynt. On the right can be seen the peaks of An Teallach (The Forge), a great attraction for climbers. To its left is Beinn Ghobhlach which looks down on its far side upon Ullapool and Loch Broom.
Once you know it is there, Mellon Udrigle can be identified when viewed from Achiltibuie on a good day.

The road continues to Poolewe and the renowned gardens at Inverewe. It then climbs around Loch Ewe ("Isle of Ewe" is still childishly amusing) down to Altbea and then Laide where there is an easily missed turn off to Mellon Udrigle, a lovely beach with a very Hebridean feel. The view is straight across to Achiltibuie which can seem quite confusing until one gets one's bearings. The Stornoway Ullapool ferry can sometimes be seen passing by in the distance. It is a stunning spot, now

Road to Gruinard 50 x 60 cm 2012
The road through First Coast and Second Coast before climbing over to Gruinard Bay.

with a basic camping site as well as some self catering wooden chalets. There is also a very tasteful Dualchas designed self catering house right on the beach.

From Laide the road passes through the quaintly named First Coast and then Second Coast before a steep climb to the stunning viewpoint above Gruinard Bay (if you can manage to stop in the small lay-by). There is another viewpoint above Little Loch Broom looking over Scoraig and to the Summer Isles. Past Dundonell an exposed but imposing moor below the mountains of An Teallach leads up past Corrieshalloch Gorge to join the main road along scenic Loch Broom to Ullapool.

Gruinard Bay   80 x 120 cm   2007
Another favourite painting of mine.

Ullapool Shore 40 x 40 cm 2011
Looking down Loch Broom.

Ullapool has always been our northern safe haven. It is a small cultural
oasis with some good shops, including two excellent bookshops
(Ullapool Bookshop and another in the Ceilidh Place), ample pubs and
eating places, a swimming pool, and another bonus in the form of the An
Talla Solais Gallery. There is even a very good (and busy) small Tesco, an
unexpected boon for the traveller. The campsite fronting Loch Broom
starts filling up late afternoon with new arrivals. There are holidaymakers
camped for a week or two but there are many travellers of all kinds:
walkers, climbers, cyclists, motorbikers, tiny tents, big tents, caravans,

Fishing Boat, Loch Broom   90 x 110 cm   2017

The campsite at Ullapool sits on the shore of Loch Broom where all types of boats pass on their way to and from the harbour, including the Stornoway ferry. Ghobhlach can be seen on the right, just above the small boat.

small campervans and big motorhomes. If you are lucky you might see what can only be described as a mobile hotel. It consists of a very large vehicle with an equally large trailer. The twenty to thirty "guests" travel and sleep in the vehicle and dine al fresco under a large tarpaulin. I believe it to be German but oddly have never seen it anywhere else. Several different nationalities are encountered in the campsite, particularly Dutch and German. It also seems very popular with visitors from the north of England. Strangely Scottish visitors aren't necessarily in the majority in the far north. The pot wash is always a good place to meet people on the campsites – we had a most interesting discussion with a German lady and a gentleman from Hull on immigration! Many of the Germans and Dutch speak ridiculously good English which merely emphasises my own (and many other Scots I suspect) very poor foreign language skills.

Ullapool is just a lovely place to wander round day or evening, including the harbour where you might see a big grey seal on the prowl. The arrival and departure of the new streamlined Stornoway ferry (*MV Loch Seaforth*) is always an event generating much activity and interest. We have seen the *Hebridean Princess* several times at Ullapool. It is a beautiful small luxury cruise ship which is based in Oban. We have spotted it in various places throughout our travels: Harris, Iona, Tiree, Gairloch, Fort William and even anchored in the bay at Tanera Mor. It would be a beautiful way to see the islands – if you can afford it. I should add that the campsite at Ullapool can be very windy and on one occasion the awning on our Bongo camper blew down at three o'clock in the morning. After collapsing the awning and piling gear on top, I tried to help another couple in trouble but they just gave up, packed their tent and drove back to Aberdeen in the darkness.

The main road continues past Ardmair and Ben Mor Coigach, and the mountains of Assynt are soon seen on the left. The turn off to Achiltibuie is easily missed. Suilven pops up spectacularly at the village of Elphin and at Loch Assynt the road seems to carry straight on to Lochinver (and also Achmelvich, Clachtoll, Stoer Head, Clashnessie

Clachtoll, 2006 – the water was cold!

Stoer Head Lighthouse, 2015 – it was windy!

and Drumbeg) while the main route north actually branches off, up to Kylesku and its beautiful bridge which sit beneath huge Quinag. It is good driving up to Scourie with very little traffic, though this may have changed in peak season with the recent promotion of the *North Coast 500 route*. After Scourie there is a small turn off to Tarbet and the bird sanctuary on Handa Island (skuas, puffins, guillemots etc). At Rhiconich the road becomes single track up to Durness. There is also a turn off to Kinlochbervie with its large fish handling depot and it then continues as a very narrow road to the beautiful beach at Oldshoremore. For the enthusiastic Sandwood Bay is a long walk further on. I confess to not having been there as it also requires walking back!

The small village of Durness is approached along the Kyle of Durness. For anyone new to the area the number of beautiful, pristine and empty beaches to be found on this coast will come as a great surprise. Durness itself is a scattering of houses, probably most famous for its proximity to Cape Wrath, the most north-westerly point on the British mainland. The nearby Balnakeil Craft Village, a former military base, is well known especially for the *Cocoa Mountain* cafe and chocolaterie.

Clachtoll   100 x 130 cm   2010

The tiny crofting township of Clachtoll lies north of Lochinver on a fairly tortuous road. Apart from the beautiful beach with distinctive headland, there is a ranger hut, ice house and old salmon bothy beside the bay. There is also a popular campsite though I am not brave enough to tackle that road with a caravan! On the other side of the rocky headland is another small beach with views to the Coigach peninsula.

Further up the coast is the Point of Stoer lighthouse. The road continues twisting and turning via Clashnessie to the pretty village of Drumbeg and back to the main road at Kylesku.

The Old Salmon Bothy   30 x 60 cm   2016

South, Achiltibuie Distant   80 x 120 cm   2012

Clachtoll Sea   73 x 92 cm   2017

North West Coast   73 x 92 cm   2017

A few miles from the Point of Stoer lighthouse.

Oldshoremore Sea   80 x 120 cm   2010

Further on from Kinlochbervie lies Oldshoremore. Surprisingly arrival is at a car park with a small public toilet and there is a graveyard alongside. A walk through a wooden gate leads over a small hillock to another gate on to the beach.

I have come across several graveyards in the highlands and islands located next to beaches, such as Balnakeil further north and Luskentyre on the Isle of Harris.

Durness campsite is a special favourite of mine. It sits directly on the cliff top above Sango Beach. It has a steady through-put of all sorts of travellers but is very quiet during the day. We once saw a remarkable vehicle, designed more for the African bush and with its own generator, while on its world tour. I remember a young family with three children in a fairly small tent pitched near the cliff edge who ate all their meals, while wearing their anoraks, on a fold-out picnic table and bench set. Fortunately it didn't rain. The site is exposed and can be very windy. We had to help a newly arrived group of young girls from Glasgow who hadn't a clue how to pitch a tent in such conditions – they didn't even have a mallet. I should add that rock pegs and a heavy mallet or hammer are essential in these areas. Those nice little pegs that come with tents are no use at all in the shallow soil. The campsite showers at Durness are not the best, but the pot wash I love as it has a corrugated tin roof and is open to the elements – atmospheric one might say.

Nearby is Balnakeil Bay with its spectacular beach and is overlooked by the impressive Balnakeil House which dates back to the 13th century. The house was rebuilt in the 1700s and a few years ago was converted into luxury self catering. There is a good walk out to the headland (Faraid Head) where we have seen puffins on a large sea stack.

A short distance to the east from Durness village is Smoo Cave, a popular tourist stop, and there are other very quiet beaches at Lerinmore, Sangobeg and Ceannabeinne within a few miles.

Better late than never, I must make special mention Fort William. It is somewhere we have always treated as a comfortable transition point in journeys between south and north. We have stayed many times at the Glen Nevis campsite, just below the Ben itself – a temporary home from home. There is good walking in the glen and it is always entertaining to watch those hardy souls setting off up the Ben and subsequently staggering back several hours later.

North West (Balnakeil)   70 x 100 cm   2011

At low tide the rock promontory seen here can be walked round to directly reach the second beach. Otherwise there is a path, just seen on the right, which leads through the spectacular dune system either on to the other beach or out to Faraid Head.

Balnakeil   50 x 60 cm   2009
Balnakeil House and its commanding view over the beach.

Green Wave   30 x 30 cm   2012

Durness Window   30 x 30 cm   2009

Durness Landscape   60 x 90 cm   2009

Clouds over Sango Bay   60 x 90 cm   2012
On a clear day the Orkney Isles can be seen beyond the headland.

Morning Sun   50 x 50 cm   2012
A dazzling very early morning on Sango beach.

Sango Beach
70 x 75 cm   2007

Sango Morning
40 x 40 cm   2011
North facing, I found the most
dramatic light at Sango Bay was in
the morning.

North Coast   70 x 100 cm   2012

Ceannabeinne, a very quiet beach a few miles from Durness. There is worthwhile walk with information boards around a ruined township nearby.

Jumping in the Waves   30 x 40 cm   2005
Ceannabeinne beach.

Postscript

I am very fortunate to have spent the past 26 years earning a living from doing what I love. There may be a certain lack of financial security which is discomforting at times – but with these things there is always a trade off required.

Painting is a huge part of my life and I am able to indulge myself within reason and more than most, but one must retain perspective. My life style has allowed me to be flexible enough to take time to deal with life's more important situations, namely health and welfare of family and others, and particularly spending my life with my wife Mary.

It has also allowed me to link my work with my love of the Scottish landscape, a rare privilege.

Tobermory to Kilchoan
ferry, 2016